Alexander
McQUEEN

GENIUS OF A GENERATION

KRISTIN KNOX

gettyimages®

A & C BLACK • LONDON

First published in Great Britain in 2010
A & C Black Publishers Limited
36 Soho Square
London W1D 3QY
www.acblack.com

ISBN 978-14081-3076-6

First edition published in 2010
Reprinted five times in 2010

CIP Catalogue records for this book are available from the British Library and the US Library of Congress.

Typeset in 10.5 on 14pt FB Californian
Book design by Susan McIntyre
Cover design by James Watson
Commissioning Editor: Susan James
Picture research: Pat Lyttle at Getty Images

Printed and Bound by Star Standard Pte Ltd, Singapore.

This book is produced using paper that is made from wood grown in managed, sustainable forests. It is natural, renewable and recyclable. The logging and manufacturing processes conform to the environmental regulations of the country of origin.

Many of the images within this book have been kindly supplied courtesy of Chris Moore and Maxine Millar of CATWALKING. COM. Thank you for all your help in making this happen.

Image Credits

Cover image by Francois Guillot AFP/GETTY IMAGES
Back cover image by Francois Guillot AFP/GETTY IMAGES

p.3 image by Francois Guillot AFP/GETTY IMAGES; p.5 (top to bottom): image by CATWALKING; image by Antonio de Moraes/WIREIMAGE/GETTY IMAGES; image by Francois Guillot AFP/GETTY IMAGES; image by Dominique Charriau/WIREIMAGE/GETTY IMAGES. p.6 image by Biasion Studio/WIREIMAGE/GETTY IMAGES; p.8 image by UK Press/GETTYIMAGES; p.9 images (top) by Jim Watson AFP/GETTYIMAGES, (bottom) by Dave M. Benett/GETTYIMAGES; p.10 image by Eric Ryan/GETTYIMAGES; p.11 image by CATWALKING; p.12 image by Pierre Verdy AFP/GETTYIMAGES; p.13 images (top) by Rabbani and Solimene WIREIMAGE/GETTYIMAGES, (bottom) by Oli Scarff/GETTYIMAGES; p.14 image by Randy Brooke/WIREIMAGE/GETTYIMAGES; p.15 images by CATWALKING; p.16 image by Hugo Philpott AFP/GETTYIMAGES; p.17 image by Francois Guillot AFP/GETTY IMAGES; p.19. image by Ben Stansall/GETTYIMAGES; p.20 image by Pascal Le Segretain/GETTYIMAGES; pp.21-23 image by Andrew Winning AFP/GETTYIMAGES; p. 24-5 images by Paul Vicente AFP/GETTYIMAGES; p.26 image by Pierre Verdy AFP/GETTYIMAGES; p.27 image by Jean Pierre Muller AFP/GETTYIMAGES; p.28. image by Sinead Lynch AFP/GETTYIMAGES; p.29. image by CATWALKING; pp.30-2 images by Hugo Philpott AFP/GETTYIMAGES; p.33. image by CATWALKING; pp.34–5 images by Martyn Hayhow AFP/GETTYIMAGES; pp.36-7 image by Petre Buzoianu/Avantis/Time & Life/GETTYIMAGES; pp.38–48 images by CATWALKING; p.49 image by Jean Pierre Muller AFP/GETTYIMAGES; pp.50-2 images by Mike Marsland WIREIMAGE/GETTYIMAGES; p.53 image by Nicholas Asfouri AFP/GETTYIMAGES; pp.54-6 images by Pierre Verdy AFP/GETTYIMAGES; pp.57-8 images by CATWALKING; pp.59–60 image by Francois Guillot AFP/GETTY IMAGES; p.61 image by Eric Ryan/GETTYIMAGES; pp.62-6 images by CATWALKING; p.67 image by Francois Guillot AFP/GETTY IMAGES; p.68 image by Biasion Studio WIREIMAGE/GETTYIMAGES; p.69 images by Francois Guillot AFP/GETTY IMAGES; pp. 70-1 images by Giuseppe Cacace/GETTYIMAGES; pp.72-3 images by Alexanderk WIREIMAGE/GETTYIMAGES; pp.74-5 images by CATWALKING; pp. 76-8 image by Pierre Verdy AFP/GETTYIMAGES; pp.79-80 image by Francois Guillot AFP/GETTY IMAGES; p.81 image by CATWALKING; p.82 image by Francois Guillot AFP/GETTY IMAGES; p.83 image by Lorenzo Santini WIREIMAGE/GETTYIMAGES; pp.84-5 image by Francois Guillot AFP/GETTY IMAGES; p.86 image by CATWALKING; p.87 image by Chad Buchanan/GETTYIMAGES; p.88 image by Eric Ryan/GETTYIMAGES; p.89 image by Francois Guillot AFP/GETTY IMAGES; pp.90–92 images by Francois Guillot AFP/GETTY IMAGES; pp.93-4 images by CATWALKING; p.95 images by Francois Guillot AFP/GETTY IMAGES; pp.96-7 images by CATWALKING; pp.98-9 images by Francois Guillot AFP/GETTY IMAGES; p.100 image by CATWALKING; p.101 image by Antonio de Moraes WIREIMAGE/GETTYIMAGES; pp 102-4 images by Francois Guillot AFP/GETTY IMAGES; p.105 image by Eric Ryan/GETTYIMAGES; pp.106-7 images by Francois Guillot AFP/GETTY IMAGES; p.108 image by Pascal Le Segretain/GETTYIMAGES; p.109 image by Antonio de Moraes WIREIMAGE/GETTYIMAGES; p.110 image by Dominique Charriau WIREIMAGE/GETTYIMAGES; p.111-2 images by Francois Guillot AFP/GETTY IMAGES; p.113-4 image by Eric Ryan/GETTYIMAGES; p.115 image by Francois Guillot AFP/GETTY IMAGES; p.116 image by Victor Boyko/GETTYIMAGES; p.117 image by CATWALKING; pp.118–120 images by Victor Boyko/GETTYIMAGES; p.121 image by Antonio de Moraes WIREIMAGE/GETTYIMAGES; p.122 image by Giuseppe Cacace AFP/GETTYIMAGES; pp.124-8 images by CATWALKING

CONTENTS

INTRODUCTION   7

GALLERY   21

Spring/Summer 1995   21

Fall/Winter 1996   22

Fall/Winter 1998   24

Fall/Winter 1999: Givenchy *Haute Couture*   26

Spring/Summer 2000: Givenchy *Haute Couture*   27

Spring/Summer 2000   28

Fall/Winter 2000   28

Spring/Summer 2001   30

Fall/Winter 2001   33

Spring/Summer 2002   36

Fall/Winter 2002   38

Spring/Summer 2003   42

Fall/Winter 2003   44

2004 American Express Show   50

Spring/Summer 2004   54

Fall/Winter 2004   57

Spring/Summer 2005   62

Fall/Winter 2005   66

Spring/Summer 2006   66

Spring/Summer 2006 Menswear   70

Fall/Winter 2006   72

Spring/Summer 2007   74

Fall/Winter 2007   79

Spring/Summer 2008   82

Fall/Winter 2008   91

Spring/Summer 2009   96

Fall/Winter 2009   101

Spring/Summer 2010   117

CONCLUSION: Fall/Winter 2010   123

Pictured here in 2006

INTRODUCTION

HIS was the kind of genius that only comes around once in a generation. Much more than just a fashion designer, Lee Alexander McQueen sought not only to dress the women of the world as the preceding titans of ready-to-wear such as Christian Dior or Yves Saint Laurent had, but to inspire them to epic artistic proportions, to bust fashion out of its commercial confines and reinvent its role in contemporary society. McQueen was often accused of misogyny for designs which objectified his models in a dark, twisted sexual manner (bondage, chainmail and even girls fainting upon being cinched into the most minute of corsets) or, even more frequently, attacked for producing fashions unwearable and inaccessible beyond the voyeuristic spectacles of his lavish, unorthodox runway shows with elaborate props and presentations which blurred the boundary between runway show and a new kind of installation art.

But therein lies the genius of Alexander McQueen, who in 2003 was appointed CBE as well as being named International Designer of the Year at the Council of Fashion Designer Awards, and who was named British Designer of the Year four times. For McQueen, fashion was not necessarily a means for self-expression, but a force to facilitate the opposite, much more akin to the role of 19th- and 20th-century painting and sculpture: to compel the wearer or beholder to surrender to the fantastical and sinister world of which McQueen was the sole artificer. These often surreal 'worlds' saw McQueen's aggressive aesthetic plunge into the darkest recesses of the soul, where themes such as witchcraft, rape and capital punishment were unearthed and then recast into things of sartorial beauty. He was the industry's aptly named *enfant terrible*, a visionary who never lost his sense of child-like wonder and curiosity, whose appetite remained unchecked by commercial ambitions – an artist in every sense of the word.

Beyond just vision, McQueen was a figure of extraordinary sartorial prowess. And without his exceptional tailoring skills – a ripe combination of both training and talent – his visions would have remained just that: dreams unable to be realized in three-dimensional form on the runway, or in stores, or eventually on the streets, illustrations forever confined to the pages of the designer's sketchbook. Trained on London's legendary Savile Row, the home of bespoke tailoring, McQueen's masterful wielding of needle and thread allowed him to execute his *avant-garde* designs with such exceptional craftsmanship that his ready-to-wear collections often exuded *haute couture* sensibility.

He was born on March 17, 1969, in Stepney in London's East End – the youngest of six children born to a taxi driver and social science teacher – and he grew up in a council flat. Because of his brash personality and humble upbringing, McQueen's identity in the fashion world was in part that of 'the outsider' who had accidentally wrangled his way into the innermost fold. The young McQueen, a creative with a flair for fashion and a penchant for the eccentric from the age of three (when he drew pictures of Cinderella in elaborate ballgowns on his sister's bedroom wall), was always an outsider at home as well. Openly gay from a young age, he was spurned by his father, bullied and teased at school. But encouraged by his mother Joyce, to whom he was very close until her death a few days before his own, the young Lee McQueen spent his time escaping into his own world, daydreaming and drawing women's clothes.

In 1985, aged 16, McQueen left school with just a single O-level and one A-level, both in Art. The next year, after seeing a television advertisement highlighting the shortage of apprentices in the tailoring business, McQueen walked into Anderson & Sheppard on Savile Row, tailor to the Prince of Wales, and was hired on the spot.

Here McQueen's aesthetic truly began to develop as his natural capacity for the chalk and scissors allowed him to quickly conquer classic cuts and shapes, like the gentleman's suit. He moved on to greater challenges such as reconstructing period tailoring, reaching back even to 16th-century pattern cutting, influences which have remained consistent throughout his body of design work. Despite having taken up residence in one of the world's most conservative sartorial outposts, McQueen still found a space to express, explore and experiment with the boundaries of his rebellious nature. For example, while still at Anderson & Sheppard, he infamously sewed a particularly offensive affront into the lining of a jacket that he had tailored for Prince Charles. As fate would have it, ten years later in 2001, the Prince of Wales returned McQueen's lewd gesture with a more gracious one of his own; he presented the designer with his third British Designer of the Year Award.

McQueen then left Anderson & Sheppard to work down the street at Gieves & Hawkes and thence to theatrical costumiers Angels and Bermans, whose influence continued to make itself felt in his creation of over-the-top, almost operatically grand, costume pieces. These were enormously popular with pop artists and musicians right from the commencement of his career – Icelandic singer Björk wore an early design for the cover of her album *Homogenic* and David Bowie sported McQueen's distressed Union Jack coat on the cover of his 1997 album *Earthling* – right up to the end when Lady Gaga stomped around in a pair of the gold Armadillo 12-inch platforms from McQueen's Spring/Summer 2010 collection in her video for the smash hit *Bad Romance*.

After departing Angels and Bermans at the tender age of 20, McQueen spent a period of time working for the Japanese designer Koji Tatsuno before traveling to Milan to work for Italian designer Romeo Gigli as a pattern cutter. In 1992, the young but now seasoned tailor returned to London at last ready to launch his own label. He completed a postgraduate course at Central St. Martin's College of Art and Design at the behest of the Head of Masters who caught a glimpse of McQueen's exceptional portfolio when he arrived at the college to tutor in pattern cutting. This was a most serendipitous encounter – it led to McQueen's discovery by (and subsequent friendship with and high-profile mentorship by) aristocratic style guru and former Fashion Editor of *Vogue*, Isabella Blow.

While McQueen always had the raw talent, the roughness of his gap-toothed East London character and often abrasive rudeness of his vision necessitated a go-between, a fashion industry veteran to reign him back where necessary and help round off the edges. Essentially, Blow assisted the young genius in finding

Fit for a McQueen: HRH Prince Charles and Alexander McQueen at the British Fashion Awards at London's Somerset House in 2001.

his footing commercially while ensuring that he stayed true to his original vision. She eventually purchased the whole of McQueen's graduate collection, buying just one item a month and paying the young designer £100 per week. 'He'd bring an outfit in a bin liner,' Blow explained to *Time Out* in 2005, 'I'd look at it and then he'd come to the cash-point with me.' She convinced him to adopt his middle name, Alexander, as the forename for his label instead of his given name of Lee, and she introduced him to key industry players. Suddenly, the Alexander McQueen brand was born.

In May 2007, Isabella Blow tragically took her own life. This was a devastating loss for the designer, who told *W Magazine* in 2008 that her death 'left a big void in my life.' In memoriam, McQueen dedicated his Spring/Summer 2008 show at Paris Fashion Week to her, sending out enormous poster-sized invitations depicting the late Blow riding to heaven in a chariot pulled by two Pegasi and integrating the theme of birds (symbolizing Blow) into his designs.

Björk flashes a smile almost as brilliant as the crystals adorning her face at the Fashion Rocks event in 2003.

Lady Gaga dedicated to McQueen her performance at the 2010 Brit Awards, which took place in London just five days after he passed away. Lady Gaga is pictured here wearing a black letter-jacket embossed with an 'M' and two crosses in tribute to his memory.

Isabella Blow champions her young *protégé* from the front row of his Fall/Winter 2004 show in Paris. 'My relationship with McQueen began in 1994,' she told *Time Out* in 2005, 'when I went to a Saint Martin's graduate show. I couldn't get a seat, so I sat on the stairs and I was just watching, when I suddenly thought: I really like those clothes, they are amazing. It was his first collection. It was the tailoring and the movement which initially drew me to them.'

RIGHT McQueen's 'bumsters' are an example of the influence of his runway collection on street style. The low-slung pants as shown here on the catwalk launched the controversial trend of low-rise jeans which became an integral part of the youth street culture for the duration of the nineties and into the noughties. Pictured here is a manifestation of the bumster from the Spring/Summer 2001 show in Paris. Image courtesy of CATWALKING.COM

McQueen exploded onto the international fashion scene with subversive designs such as the controversial 'Highland Rape' collection of 1995, which was stitched together from left-over scraps of fabric. He designed the aptly-named low-slung craze-igniting 'bumster' trousers. The great spectacle of his Fall/Winter 1998 show in London was a woman in a red rubber hooded catsuit standing at the center of a burning ring of fire. Just two years after meeting Isabella Blow, he was named British Designer of the Year (the first of four times this honour would be bestowed on him) and was headhunted by Bernard Arnault, chairman of LVMH Moët Hennessy Louis Vuitton, to follow in the footsteps of fellow Englishman (and son of a London plumber) John Galliano and head up creative direction at the flagging French fashion house of Givenchy. He was just 27 years old at the time.

Though initially unenthused at the prospect of streamlining his own vision to sync with the French brand's heritage, McQueen eventually accepted the position as an opportunity to further establish his design expertise and cultivate his profile on the international scene. But the partnership was tumultuous from the start as Givenchy's brand, the ultimate in understated Parisian elegance whose founder was couturier to Audrey Hepburn, was just so radically different from the agenda of the young Alexander McQueen who sent space aliens down the Parisian runways to the great distaste of the press and buyers. In the end, he refused to compromise his creative vision to suit the French house and spoke unfavorably of the brand and its founder, Hubert de Givenchy, to the press.

'It was just money to me,' McQueen, always frank, reflected to the *Guardian* in 2005. 'But there was nothing I could do: the only way it would have worked would have been if they had allowed me to change the whole concept of the house, to give it a new identity, and they never wanted me to do that.'

After five years, McQueen and Givenchy parted ways because the headstrong designer complained that his contract with the French label and its parent conglomerate was 'constraining his creativity' and that their demand

Carla Bruni, when she was commanding catwalks instead of affairs of state as France's fashionable first lady, walks the runway in a traditional evening gown at Givenchy *Haute Couture* Fall/Winter 1997. The gown's long, sweeping lines reference founder Hubert de Givenchy's designs for Audrey Hepburn in the film *Breakfast at Tiffany's*, but the crystal-encrusted, somewhat futuristic, star adorning the shoulder, and the sweeping Swarovski milky-way across the body of the dress, are very much McQueen's aesthetic.

for the production of six collections per year simply did not allow for any creative innovation or evolution to occur within the brand. 'Give me time and I'll give you revolutionary,' he told the *New York Times* in 2001.

If time was what McQueen needed to instigate revolution, after leaving Givenchy and returning to his own eponymous label with the help of the Gucci group, LVMH's rival (which acquired a 51% stake in the business), he finally got what he wanted. He was at last able to come into his own, to embark upon a quest for the truly revolutionary.

In a few short seasons, McQueen succeeded in building a global fashion empire according to his own vision, and became a red-carpet favorite amongst Hollywood and international A-listers – Sarah Jessica Parker, Naomi Cambell, Lady Gaga and Kate Moss are counted amongst his friends and biggest fans. He opened five stand-alone stores in London, New York, Los Angeles, Milan and Las Vegas, launched a secondary diffusion label – McQ – and pioneered a now-iconic skull print motif which became an instant must-have accessory in every form, from chiffon scarves and jewellery to bags. He even collaborated with major American retail chain Target in February 2009, to resounding fiscal success.

At last McQueen was in his element and had an adequate financial structure in place to realize his dreams – his imagination was finally truly unleashed. And nowhere did it run riot more than on his catwalks, which have been one of the main highlights of Paris Fashion Week since he began showing there in 2000 (he had previously shown in London and New York). These shows drew on a cabinet of inspirations ranging from the macabre to the bizarre: Hitchcock heroines, mental asylums, *Lord Of The Flies*, dark and twisty carnivals, and evolution in a post-Apocalyptic landscape among them. '[They're] my own living nightmares,' he quipped to the *Guardian* in 2005. For his Spring 2003 collection McQueen recreated a shipwreck; in Spring 2005 he made a human chess game; and for Autumn 2006, Kate Moss (immediately following the disgrace of her 2005 drugs scandal) was beamed onto the runway as a life-sized holograph, a vulnerable apparition, eerily clad in ghostly rippling masses of gauzy white fabric.

One show (Spring/Summer 1999) famously saw model Shalom Harlow clad all in white and turned into

Actress Sarah Jessica Parker pictured here with Alexander McQueen on the red carpet at the Costume Institute Gala at the Metropolitan Museum of Art in New York in 2006. Their matching tartans are in keeping with the theme of that evening's event, the opening of the exhibit *Anglomania: Tradition and Transgression in British Fashion.*

Alexander McQueen flagship store on Bond Street in London. Despite being a celebrity favorite, he never courted the rich and famous as clientele. He once half-joked of socialite Paris Hilton to the *Independent* in April 2008, when opening a flagship store in Los Angeles, 'If she comes past the shop, hopefully she'll just keep walking.'

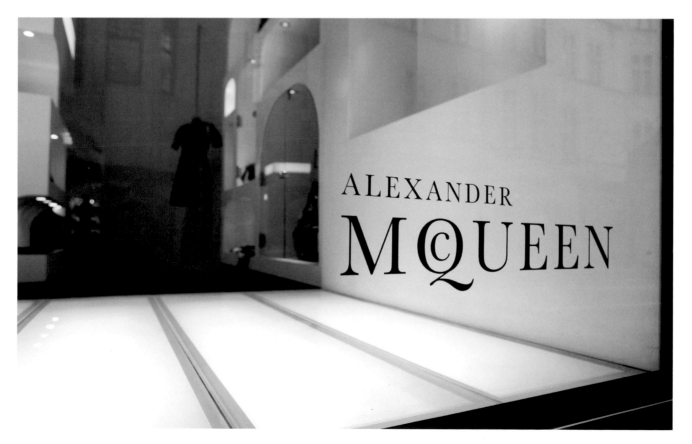

The eerie three-dimensional holograph of Kate Moss, at the Fall/Winter 2006 show, hovered momentarily above the runway before disappearing, like a phantom on a solitary road. This dream-like fragility underscored with a touch of cynicism really exemplifies one of the key tensions in McQueen's work.

Model Shalom Harlow acts as both muse and canvas as the Spring/ Summer 1999 show as two flanking robots pelt her white strapless dress with paint. Image courtesy of CATWALKING.COM

BELOW Models pose inside the giant glass box for the finale, placing their hands on the glass as if longing to escape the asylum in which they are contained. Image courtesy of CATWALKING.COM

The curvaceous model in the box strikes a pose reminiscent of Botticelli, reclining on a horned wrought iron couch as moths rest on her legs and body at the Spring/Summer 2000 show in London.

a human canvas as she was spray-painted *à la* Jackson Pollock live on stage by two robotic arms adapted from a car factory. Another show (Spring/Summer 2001) took place inside a mirrored cube, which, when illuminated, looked like a holding cell in a mental institution. The models wore hospital headbands and one sported a huge feather creation with stuffed eagles dangling from a mobile-like device over her head; the cuckoo's nest broken and defunct, with no escape, actualized on a fashion catwalk.

The Spring/Summer 2001 show wrapped by revealing another cube within the psychiatric ward masquerading as runway, in which lay a large woman (considerably bigger than the other models) reclining nude, her face covered by an iron mask adjoined to a network of plastic breathing tubes. Moths fluttered within, the final accent on the twisted and sinister Francis-Bacon-meets-Sigmund-Freud theme running throughout the sublime presentation.

And while, year after year, his shows became the spectacles of the fashion week season, unlike his contemporaries McQueen was insistent that the emphasis remain on the garments themselves and refused to dip into the commercial machine of celebrity in order to publicize himself and his clothes. In 1999, McQueen refused to invite then-Spice Girl Victoria Beckham to his London show because he believed her celebrity would overshadow the appearance of Aimee Mullins, the Paralympic athlete who as a child had had both legs amputated from the knee down, who was scheduled to showcase hand-carved cherry-wood prosthetics designed by McQueen alongside the rest of his models.

In September 2009, McQueen produced a truly spectacular runway show of epic proportions in Paris, which would turn out to be the last he attended. The Spring/Summer 2010 collection was entitled *Plato's Atlantis* and it touched on socially-poignant themes including climate change and evolution; some of the clothes whispered of potential biological hybridization of women with sea mammals in the post-biological-meltdown future.

'I thought that his Spring/Summer 2010 show was the pinnacle of his career,' remembers British Designer and McQueen contemporary Amanda Wakeley. 'A theatrical spectacle which presented a collection of immaculately-produced looks.'

A model exits the catwalk at the *Plato's Atlantis* show in October 2010 in Paris

It was an expression through fashion of McQueen's eschatological forecast of the world's ecological Armageddon, his take on the global climate crisis; life on earth began in the oceans, and perhaps it will indeed be a watery end for man. In terms of the fashions carrying the message, the collection's futuristic reptile-skin-printed micro-minis resembled something akin to a cockroach or other form of insect magnified under a microscope. They were layered over watery-graphic-print leggings and teamed with the enormous – now iconic – 'Armadillo' 12-inch hoof-like scaly python platforms and 10-inch melted metallic plastic-meets-nuclear-waste 'Alien' shoes (three of the models refused to wear them for fear of becoming runway wreckage and for the safety of their delicate frames). These designs were proof positive that the designer had just begun to explore the deepest troves of his imagination; the treasures of possibility had just begun to escape the recesses of his psyche and, subsequently, materialize on the global fashion stage.

September's spectacle was more than just a monumental sartorial achievement, it was also one of the first runway shows to be streamed live from Fashion Week on the internet (on SHOWstudio.com,), giving industry outsiders 'front row' access to the catwalk. After Lady Gaga Twittered the exciting news, the site was rushed by so many users that it crashed, thus demonstrating McQueen's tremendous resonance with the populous beyond the fashion industry's insider-only ivory towers. Come the Autumn/Winter 2010 shows, every major designer from New York to Milan to Tokyo (including Prada, Vivienne Westwood and Burberry) streamed their shows live online. Advertisements splashed around Bryant Park at New York Fashion Week in February 2010 claimed boldly that 'video is the new black.'

McQueen was ever the forward thinker, and unlike many of his contemporaries never felt threatened by the changing landscape of media, with the advent of social networks such as Facebook and Twitter gaining commercial footing and influence in the corporate sphere. McQueen joined Twitter in September 2009, just before his show, and posted messages regularly. McQueen saw the advent of new media and the ascent of the internet as a means to further spread his vision abroad and reach a new, wider and even more international audience. When *Women's Wear Daily* asked about the live-streaming of his show, the plucky

McQueen answered matter-of-factly, 'Really, what I'm aiming for is world domination!'

McQueen's mother, Joyce, died on February 2, 2010 just nine days before the designer tragically took his own life in his London flat on February 11. He was only 40 years old and due to show his Fall/Winter 2010 collection in Paris on March 9, 2010. News of the designer's tragic demise rocked the global fashion community, which had just come together for New York Fashion Week. Anna Wintour, editor in chief of American *Vogue* and one of McQueen's earliest supporters, bolted pale-faced from her front row seat at the BCBG Max Azria show upon receiving the news via text message. 'In such a short career, Alexander McQueen's influence was astonishing – from street style, to music culture and the world's museums. His passing marks an insurmountable loss,' she told the *Financial Times*.

British Fashion Council Chairman Harold Tillman opened London Fashion Week, following on the heels of the New York shows and taking place just six days after McQueen's suicide, with a minute of silence in tribute to the late designer.

'He proved that this industry and this city is one of opportunity, he left school with one O-Level and, with a good mix of determination, hard work and genius, he became and will remain one of London's leading lights,' Mr. Tillman told the *Times*. 'He has inspired so many to follow and establish their own collection and has influenced many designers. To ensure London, his home city, continues to grow as a global fashion centre will be a fitting tribute to this brilliant man.'

'The way Alexander McQueen fused his Savile Row tailoring discipline and skills with a very modern approach to cutting was both remarkable and truly inspirational,' remarked Amanda Wakeley. 'He was a true, gritty Brit with an extraordinary talent.'

While the industry and indeed the general public mourned the loss of one the greatest creatives of our time – laying flowers, letters, poems and candles outside his shops – the future of his business and the Alexander McQueen label, a vision robbed of its visionary, was for a time uncertain. Unlike the major financial success stories under the Gucci Group's umbrella (Balenciaga or Stella McCartney, for example), the Alexander McQueen label had always had a less-than-charmed fiscal existence and was not profitable until 2007. Even then, its success was predominantly due to a prudent use of licensing.

Show-goers at London Fashion Week, which began February 18th, 2010, scribbled notes and posted photos and mementos in honor of the fallen fashion designer on a board in the central media area of Somerset House, the official British Fashion Council-run venue of London Fashion Week.

So amongst speculations of shuttering and the cancellation of a McQ presentation in New York scheduled to take place just 24 hours after his death, François-Henri Pinault, PPR executive chairman (which owns Gucci Group) announced a week after McQueen's passing that the eponymous fashion label would indeed live to see another season, and would take design direction from a new creative director.

And so it seems that the proverbial show will go on. Although McQueen's death left industry insiders wondering whether a label which is so heavily steeped in its creator's imagination, and whose brand DNA is that of its flesh and blood designer, could indeed survive without its dark knight dreaming his twisted and magically nightmarish dreams at its helm, McQueen's legacy has superseded the man. And though McQueen himself has departed from the ateliers of Paris, the momentum created by his aspirations for world domination continues. His imagination and his creative spirit have metamorphosed, just like theme of the hybrid-sea creatures of his final runway collection, and they will live on to compel, shock and inspire another generation to dream the dream that is fashion.

A show-stopping evening gown from the Fall/Winter 2009 collection.

GALLERY

Spring/Summer 1995

A model displays a liquid metallic floor-length gown at McQueen's
Spring/Summer 1995 collection shown in London. This is an early
incarnation of the fencing mask, a motif which at first shocked
McQueen's audience but came to be regarded as one of his
trademarks; he continually revisited and reworked it across different
collections over the years.

Fall/Winter 1996

A model sports antlers as a headpiece during McQueen's Fall/Winter 1996 runway show at London Fashion Week. This look is an early demonstration of McQueen's costume tendencies and his engagement with elaborate headgear. Later in his career, in order to produce more and more extravagant hats to complement his runway collections, McQueen teamed up with eccentric British milliner, Philip Treacy.

A model peeks through the gap in the high collar of the super-structured embroidered bodice from the Fall/Winter 1996 show at London Fashion Week. This look demonstrates McQueen's mastery as a tailor and reflects his omnipresent fascination with avant-garde tailoring, specifically as it relates to period costume.

Fall/Winter 1998

The runway extravaganza that was the Fall/Winter 1998 show is a prime example of McQueen's tremendous sense of showmanship. Despite being at the helm of Givenchy in Paris at this time, McQueen continued showing his eponymous label in London. In this infamous runway extravaganza, a model wearing a red hooded catsuit seems to emerge as a creature of flame from within a giant ring of fire, burning live on stage.

RIGHT In this close up from the same collection, with the model clad in a red snakeskin dress, you can see how McQueen has co-ordinated the hair and makeup to enhance this vision of a Satanic serpent. The model's hair, finely braided and twisted, is reminiscent of a snake's coil and she has red demon eyes – a fine example of McQueen's extraordinary attention to every last detail.

Fall/Winter 1999 / Givenchy Haute Couture

A mannequin with a lit plexiglass head appeared on the catwalk, rising up from underneath the runway on a platform to present a daywear look at McQueen's Fall/Winter 1999 show in Paris for Givenchy Haute Couture. With its caramel tones and floral brocade top teamed with Mary Jane shoes, the look channels the 1940s.

Spring/Summer 2000 / Givenchy Haute Couture

A look from McQueen's Spring/Summer 2000 Haute Couture collection for Givenchy, on show in Paris, which illustrates the struggle the designer faced in integrating his vision with that of the French house. In this example, McQueen's own style can be seen in the plunge-front neckline of the impeccably tailored jacket, especially since it is here rendered in an unusual pearly metallic hue, the very same iridescent shade that walked on his final runway a decade later. The pleated trousers are more in line with the House of Givenchy's traditional design aesthetic. In this particular instance, the marriage between McQueen and Givenchy is a success and the look exudes a classic French elegance with an unexpected British twist.

Spring/Summer 2000

A model works McQueen's Spring/
Summer 2000 runway in one of the early
manifestations of his rigid body-contoured
corsets, now an instantly recognizable
McQueen trademark which, by the end of
his career, evolved to levels of sophistication
impressive for such a simple concept. The
harsh nakedness of the corset is offset by
softness of the hand-ruched *appliqué* rose
drop-waist skirt, carefully wrought with
couture richness.

Fall/Winter 2000

RIGHT A model walks the runway at the Fall/
Winter 2000 show displaying a rare and
unusual example of dramatic knitwear in
a McQueen collection. Image courtesy of
CATWALKING.COM

Spring/Summer 2001

British supermodel Erin O'Connor models a fantastical avian-inspired evening dress at the legendary 'Birds' Spring/Summer 2001 show in London, where McQueen seated the audience around a giant mirrored box meant to evoke the troubled setting of a mental asylum. While some looks touched on the disturbing uniform staples of such institutions (suggestive bandaging and nurses' wear), others, such as this dress, brought to life the hopeful visual of flying over and *out* of the cuckoo's nest.

Another look from the Spring/Summer 2001 show, encapsulating
both the avian and asylum themes of the collection. The taxidermy
eagles seem to be swooping on the feather-skirted model, either
in aggressive attack or perhaps serene rescue. The bandage-
style headband framing her face links back to the theme of the
psychiatric hospital and the feather-adorned skirt underscores the
collection's references to Hitchcock's 1963 film, *The Birds*.

Yet another articulation of the bird theme in the Spring/Summer 2001 collection. This shift, adorned with large plumes, nearly overwhelms the tiny frame of the model, her arms outstretched like a baby bird about to take wing.

Fall/Winter 2001

A model wears a Chinese-inspired ensemble at the Fall/Winter 2001 show in London. Set to the tune of a children's festival, and complete with a merry-go-round, in this show McQueen sought to expose the sinister side of the circus, where a clown could be viewed as a thing of comic amusement or nightmarish terror. To this effect, the models moved about an eerie backdrop of enormous taxidermy lions and tigers, abandoned toys and defunct circus paraphernalia, a set which perfectly encapsulated McQueen's aesthetic of the disturbed child inside – the darkness within the dream. Image courtesy of CATWALKING. COM

A model displays a splendid gold-painted fox skeleton-wrap,
part of the Fall/Winter 2001 collection and a prime example of
McQueen's remanipulation of the macabre into a thing of true
exquisite beauty.

McQueen was one of the first amongst the great contemporary designers to succeed in reinventing the military look for the modern era, as he had always had a fascination with uniform tailoring from different periods and different cultures combined with an edgy rock and roll sensibility. This look from the Fall/Winter 2001 collection featured some of the early appearances of the skull motif: a seal affixed to the front of the model's helmet and stamped on the enormous belt buckle about her waist.

Spring/Summer 2002

McQueen's Spring/Summer 2002 collection, his first after signing with the Gucci Group and relocating his runway spectacles to Paris, was entitled *The Dance of the Twisted Bull* and featured a camp and vamp take on all themes Latin and Hispanic. Here a model is pictured in a tattered reimagining of a flamenco dress worn over red and white polka dotted tights for an added component of layered texture.

RIGHT This black suit from the Spring/Summer 2002 collection was McQueen's modern take on the toreador. Worn without anything underneath, the suggestive leather straps convey a hint of McQueen's telltale dark and aggressive sexual energy, which aligns nicely with the testosterone-fuelled concept of bullfighting.

Fall/Winter 2002

LEFT A purple-poncho-clad model leading two wolfish hounds opened McQueen's Fall/Winter 2002 show at Paris' La Conciergerie, the former prison of aristocrats during the French Revolution where Marie Antoinette was held before her execution. Appropriately, the collection explored the concept of incarceration. Image courtesy of CATWALKING.COM

RIGHT Playing into the somber mood of the La Conciergerie venue, the models in McQueen's Fall/Winter 2002 collection seemed to be imprisoned in a series of impossibly tailored dresses, such as this one, overwrought with dominatrix leather detailing. The ruff detail about the model's neck reinforces the link with the 18th century. Image courtesy of CATWALKING.COM

This look from the Fall/Winter 2002 collection pushes the dominatrix theme to its limits. Including sexy lingerie styled with leather bondage pieces, a facemask and thigh-high boots, this theme is high octane in its sexual drama. Image courtesy of CATWALKING.COM

RIGHT One of the final looks of McQueen's Fall/Winter 2002 show, a caped and masked model swoops onto the catwalk like one of the Three Musketeers, a strong image of female liberation in stark contrast to the women bound in skintight S&M leather and constrictive masks of the show's first movement. The arrival of a heroic figure at the show's end illustrates McQueen's inclination to present clear and easy-to-follow narratives on his runways. Image courtesy of CATWALKING.COM

Spring/Summer 2003

The Spring/Summer collection of 2003 was another showcase divided into distinct movements – pirates, shipwrecked maidens in tattered, gauzy floor-length ball gowns, and finally the rainforests and the birds-of-paradise who occupy their lush canopies. This particular look stems from references to the rainforest, an early instance of McQueen's fascination with the environment and man's detrimental effect upon it. Image courtesy of CATWALKING.COM

RIGHT This look from Spring/Summer 2003 updates and de-contextualizes McQueen's penchant for historical tailoring as a Tudor-style golden satin jacket complete with ruff is worn over a rainbow tie-dye flouncy chiffon skirt. The effect of this sharp, masculine military jacket teamed with the bright femininity of the skirt perhaps conjures up a vision of the genderbender shipwrecked characters of Shakespeare's *Twelfth Night*. Image courtesy of CATWALKING.COM

Fall/Winter 2003

A model walks McQueen's Fall/Winter 2003 runway, which was designed to look like snow-covered tundra, in a regal A-line dress with thick paneling reminiscent of Samurai armour. Two facets of traditional dress which gripped McQueen's imagination since the beginning are the regalia of the world's royals and the armies they commanded. The citation of traditional Samurai attire is reinforced by the model's hairstyle, a loose topknot. Image courtesy of CATWALKING.COM

RIGHT This lavish look from Fall/Winter 2003 seems to have a Russian folk or fairytale influence. The jacket, with its tie-dyed fox trim, is a rare use of fur by McQueen. Image courtesy of CATWALKING.COM

Another look from the Fall/Winter 2003 collection based on tradition Russian folk dress, this model looks almost doll-like. The, soft, homemade feel of the printed quilted skirt is counterbalanced by the severity of the jacket's lines. Black studded boots lend a rock and roll edge to this otherwise folksy ensemble. Image courtesy of CATWALKING.COM

In a move anticipatory of McQueen's radical Fall/Winter 2009 collection, from which the designer's funky deconstructed houndstooth and black-and-white check prints quickly attained cult status within the industry, McQueen worked a black and white check and houndstooth nip-tucked suit into this collection six years earlier, in 2003. The reference seems to balance out a collection otherwise very much steeped in the historicism of Eurasian culture. Image courtesy of CATWALKING.COM

LEFT Here the houndstooth *trompe l'oeil* fabric is folded into the shape of a mini-kimono, further underscoring the elements of East-meets-West running throughout the Fall/Winter 2003 collection. Image courtesy of CATWALKING.COM

ABOVE The finale look at the Fall/Winter 2003 show was particularly exemplary of the near pyrotechnic-level of theatrics surrounding McQueen's runway presentations. The audience gasped audibly as a model wearing a leather bodysuit hitched to a long, flowing kimono-like parachute blazed down the runway in the middle of a wind tunnel.

2004 American Express Show London (Kate Moss)

LEFT Kate Moss models one of the original skull-print looks at the American Express Black show in London's Earls Court venue in 2004. This print has since gone on to become one of McQueen's signatures, a motif reworked across collections and his accessories, with the scarves most notably becoming a cult must-have after Moss took to wearing hers religiously.

RIGHT A model all in white almost disappears into the blizzard falling softly around her at the American Express Black Show of 2004.

LEFT McQueen reaches back as far
as the Middle Ages and introduces
a show-stopping chainmail creation,
seen here on the American Express
Black runway in 2004 in the form of a
long-sleeved top worn *sans* trousers
with complete facial coverage.
McQueen returned to this motif in his
Fall/Winter 2009 collection, when it
became a layering piece worn under
ornate printed silk evening dresses.

RIGHT A model flaunts yet another
example of McQueen's trademark
leather bodysuits, riddled with cut-
outs and textured detailing, which
leaves very little to the imagination.

Spring/Summer 2004

LEFT Two models strike a dance pose during the presentation of McQueen's Spring/Summer 2004 collection, a lighthearted reenactment of Sydney Pollack's Depression-era film *They Shoot Horses, Don't They?* Taking place in the Salle Wagram, a nineteenth-century dance hall in Paris, the performance was choreographed by Scottish dancer Michael Clark and models together with professional dancers underwent over two weeks of rigorous rehearsals.

RIGHT Muted floral tones and free-flowing shapes rendered in breezy chiffon reflect a romanticism not normally associated with Depression-era style. Just as McQueen found the sinister element in the lighthearted, he unearthed the beauty buried at the heart of human adversity.

Fall/Winter 2004

For his Fall/Winter 2004 collection, McQueen declared that he intended to strip away 'all theatrics and focus purely on design.' He created a collection dominated by clean cut modern garments rendered in an array of pale-paletted neutrals, such as this simple flesh-toned, hooded jersey dress. Image courtesy of CATWALKING.COM

This Grecian-style floor-sweeping gown with crisscross bodice from McQueen's Fall/Winter 2004 collection quickly became a celebrity favorite on the red carpet. He reworked this simple yet stunning silhouette more than once. Image courtesy of CATWALKING.COM

RIGHT Despite McQueen's expressed desire to present a show devoid of spectacle in his Fall/Winter 2004 show, when the collection moved from day into eveningwear, the tone turned dramatically towards the conceptually futuristic. Here Estonian supermodel Tiiu Kuik wears an extreme rendition of the classic evening gown. Unlike many McQueen shows, the shock value in this look lies purely in the design itself and not its presentation.

Another futuristic evening look from the Fall/ Winter 2004 collection. The gaping widened collar takes this heavily embellished corset-style jacket from Tudor times to the 23rd century.

RIGHT This conceptual silhouette from Fall/ Winter 2004 seems to devour its model's head and is an early gesture towards the super-sculpted grotesquely exaggerated shapes to come on McQueen's Fall/ Winter 2008 and 2009 runways. This marks the evolution of his designs from fashions simply worn by models to designs integrated with their human carriers, becoming an organic part of them, like a second skin.

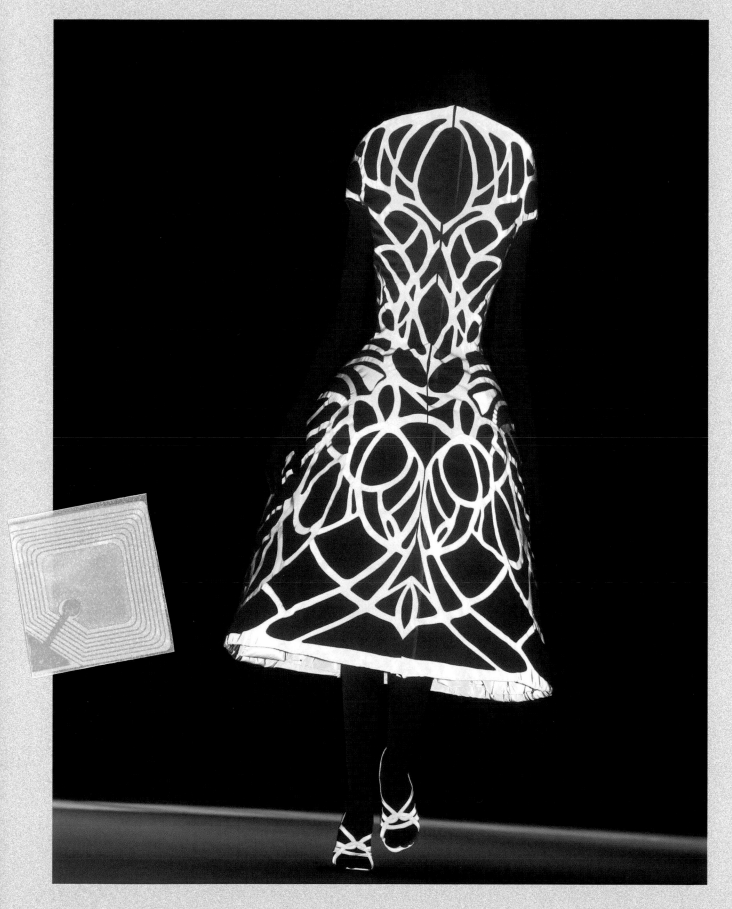

Spring/Summer 2005

Just like his Spring/Summer 2001 collection, Spring/Summer 2005 saw McQueen revisit some of his more successful moments, laying them out strategically on his giant chessboard. Here, he reworked the kimono, this time in richly-embroidered silk and including his signature plunge-front, sculpted neckline. Image courtesy of CATWALKING.COM

RIGHT McQueen here repeats the popular crisscross bodice from the previous season (Fall/Winter 2004). Gone is the floor-length goddess silhouette, instead replaced by a younger, flouncier *tulle* puffball above-the-knee skirt. Same basic concept, but totally different appeal. Image courtesy of CATWALKING.COM

This look from Spring/Summer 2005 is an amalgam of many of McQueen's more successful sartorial experiments over the years. The rigid molded corset reaches back to Spring/Summer 2000, but this version, updated with mouth brace and resembling a full body cast, references the hospital theme of the Spring/Summer 2001 collection. The wig elements in both the skirt and long ponytail suggest the garb of a Mongolian warrior and are reminiscent of McQueen's toying with traditional Asian military dress two years prior, in his Fall/Winter 2003 collection. Image courtesy of CATWALKING.COM

The carousel motif on this quilted A-line skirt from Spring/Summer 2005 looks back to the carnival theme of his Fall/Winter 2001 collection. The rigid body-molded corset cinched tightly over the dress undercuts the playful, childlike feel of the merry-go-round print, infusing the look with a sense of physical constraint, again realizing McQueen's central tension of the darkness of the child within. Image courtesy of CATWALKING.COM

Fall/Winter 2005

A model at McQueen's Fall/Winter 2005 show carries the 'Novak' bag in its debut season down the runway. Here pictured in a mock croc forest green, the 'Novak' takes its name from legendary screen actress Kim Novak, famed for her role in Alfred Hitchcock's *Vertigo*. The 'Novak,' a favourite amongst celebrities, became an instant cult classic and the brand's flagship bag which has since spawned a legion of versions varying in size, color and fabric. Image courtesy of CATWALKING.COM

Spring/Summer 2006

RIGHT Spring/Summer 2006 saw McQueen reign in his aesthetic and tone down the shock value. This more wearable look, one amongst many in a collection which kicked off with an array of black suits, denotes a shift away from his signature structured tailoring as McQueen experiments with more wearable shapes for daywear. This flippy mini-skirt, with its micro-pleating and muted color palette, may perhaps reference Japanese fashion designer, Issey Miyake, who is famed for his origami-like folds.

LEFT In the editors' notes to the Spring/Summer 2006 show,
McQueen claimed he had turned to the Greek Pantheon for his
inspiration. This white crystal-beaded gown is an unusual take on
fashion's recurring dalliance with the goddess theme, emphasizing
the filigree detail at the back instead of focusing on layers of
draped chiffon.

These two fleeting glimpses of swimwear in the Spring/Summer
2006 collection represent one of McQueen's few forays into that
realm; though they are beautiful creations, with McQueen more is
more, hence the brevity of the dalliance.

Spring/Summer 2006 Menswear

Not just a misogynist as his critics have sometimes claimed, McQueen here presents a masculine version of the skintight, overtly-sexual bodysuits which often featured in his womenswear collections.

FAR RIGHT McQueen did not shy away from dramatic experimentation even on the menswear runways of Milan. Here, a male version McQueen's recurrent 'birds' walks the Spring/Summer 2006 runway, coif mohawked and wearing a cape made of leather leaves.

Fall/Winter 2006

Model Marta Berkzkalna wears an extraordinary pheasant-feathered headpiece at McQueen's Fall/Winter 2006 runway show in Paris. The recurrent use of tartan in this collection references his scandalous debut in 1997 with 'Highland Rape,' but also serves as a barometer for how far the designer had come since his first season. Gone was the roughness of aesthetic and the crudeness of material (McQueen used fabric scraps in the original collection). Here walks a collection with Scottish nobility in its bones, Shetland fairy-tale princesses -- the stuff of fashion fantasy.

This ghostly bride clad in floor-length tiered antique lace, complete with antler headpiece, served to inspire pop sensation and fashion-icon-in-the-making, Lady Gaga, who has been seen in a similar lace dress as well as horned headgear on more than one occasion.

Spring/Summer 2007

Another beautiful and innovative example of McQueen's Edwardiana in the Spring/Summer collection of 2007. The corset here is reworked into a modern suit silhouette, yet its exaggerated framework lends the look an antique feel. Its dusty palette and floral detail at the collar and sleeve reflect a level of attention to detail on par with *couture* sensibilities. Image courtesy of CATWALKING.COM

RIGHT Staged in the round in Paris' Cirque d'Hiver, models in McQueen's Spring/Summer 2007 collection traversed the runway beneath an enormous dusty crystal chandelier to the tune of a live band, evoking a sense of the romanticism of days gone by. And while McQueen cited Barry Lyndon and Goya amongst his influences in the show's notes, his dalliance with Edwardiana reveals a unique glimpse of a softer side to fashion's dogged bad boy. This flower gown, stunning in its painstaking *couture*-level execution, despite looking as though it could have stepped right out of a rococo mural and onto the runway, still hinted at the signature McQueen toughness with its strong and sculpted shoulders, keeping the overall look feeling modern and fresh. Image courtesy of CATWALKING.COM

LEFT, AND DETAIL RIGHT This look from the Spring/Summer 2007 collection is McQueen's take on a Victorian bride. Though she is clad in white with clear bridal suggestions, the antique quality of her veil, the ashen color of which seems to coat the lace like a film of dust accumulated over years of neglect, suggests a general sentiment of something sinister lurking beneath the bridal veil. Something, perhaps, to the tune of Mary Shelly and Braham Stoker's Romanticism.

This sheer lace *appliqué* dress on McQueen's Spring/Summer 2007 runway in Paris has also inspired pop star Lady Gaga, who has performed in something very similar, though not designed by McQueen.

Fall/Winter 2007

The collection of Fall/Winter 2007 saw McQueen's infamous exploration of the theme of witchcraft come to life on the catwalk. McQueen had discovered that his mother's bloodline dated as far back as the Salem witch-hunts of the 17th century and that one of her ancestors was persecuted. Again he deploys the firmly molded bodycase, here somewhat disturbingly rendered in chocolate brown and complete with a mask, almost making the model appear as though she has been encased in bark. Gone are any signs of the previous season's flirtation with themes of light and romance. Here was McQueen's inner darkness unleashed in a way that he felt directly related to his own lineage, the dark child come out to play whilst ruminating on themes such as religious persecution, and conceptions of paganism and hell.

LEFT His creative curiosity knew no
nationalistic bounds. In his Fall/Winter 2007
collection, McQueen not only explored
notions of dark magic in a European context,
but around the world and through time.
The show's set featured an inverted pyramid
suspended over a red pentagram traced
in a black-sand circle and, with the clothes
themselves, he referenced links between
ancient Egypt and folk culture in the early
British New World.

The Egyptian influences in the collection
are clearly emphasized in this look, with the
model resembling a golden statuette of some
ancient divinity, perhaps like those squirreled
away to protect and serve the pharoahs in
the afterlife. Indeed, her texturized skintight
metallic unitard, golden breastplate and
lapis-colored eyes make her appear to be
a sarcophagus herself, sprung to life on the
runway. Image courtesy of CATWALKING.
COM

Spring/Summer 2008

McQueen's Spring/Summer 2008 collection was an homage to his late mentor and dear friend, Isabella Blow. Birds again crept into the collection, as the theme not only personally symbolized Blow to McQueen, but was also representative of his own career highlights, which would never have blossomed without her guidance. He also self-referenced other collections past during this show, including the Japanese-themed couture collection which he designed for Givenchy. This model's face is covered with appliqué feathers, and the beautiful chiffon goddess gown wisps down the runway like a delicate cloud. This look is particularly emblematic of the avian element, more dove than eagle this time around.

RIGHT Yet another manifestation of the bird, this time a creature of power and majesty as opposed to one of vulnerable innocence. Here the parachute dress juxtaposed with the eagle's feathers harks back to the original 'birds' in their Spring/Summer 2001 asylum, seven years earlier. Try as he might, it seems McQueen himself could never fly the cuckoo's nest; bird influences emerge as one of the most persistent features of his incredibly diverse collections over the years.

Two models donned fencing masks and shoulder pads to walk the runway at McQueen's Spring/Summer 2008 show in Paris, color inverses of one another. Despite the fact that the clean, modern silhouettes seemed simplistically out of place in the otherwise elaborate, over-the-top collection, they were among the best sellers of the season and spotted on many a red carpet.

RIGHT In a memorial reference to Blow and her legendary love of eccentric hats, McQueen surrounds this model's head with a bouquet of butterflies at his Spring/Summer 2008 show. The surrealist creation was the result of one of the many collaborations with British milliner, Philip Treacy.

LEFT A model wears a beautifully tie-dye printed chiffon dress, the collar accentuated with tropical-bird plumage at McQueen's Spring/Summer 2008 show in Paris. Image courtesy of CATWALKING.COM

These extreme platforms are McQueen's take on the traditional Japanese *geta*. The conceptualism of McQueen's footwear surely helped set the tone for the global rise of the 'it' or 'statement' shoe in the ensuing seasons (from Fall/Winter 2009).

Here McQueen references the *Japonisme* of some of his early work at Givenchy. The leather S&M-influenced waist-piece is a shape which he reworks and reworks over the course of his career; it accessorizes the full range of looks from adding an additional element of bondage to sexually subversive body suits to cinching the waists of the most feminine evening gowns.

Another example of McQueen's diverse hand was on display in the eclectic Spring/Summer 2008 collection. This sculpted python suit embodies McQueen's signature pristine tailoring with a modern conceptual twist. The angular shoulders and plunging neckline as an update to the modern woman's suit reach as far back as his Spring/Summer 2000 *Haute Couture* collection for Givenchy. The coiled snail shell headpiece is another of Philip Treacy's whimsical creations.

Fall/Winter 2008

LEFT One of the most iconic dresses of his most memorable collections of all time (Fall/Winter 2008), McQueen's vision of the romance and fantasy of the British Empire was one of pure sartorial perfection. Inspired by a trip to India, McQueen played upon themes both military and regal, rounding off the collection with an homage to the Hardy Aimes' 1950s British couture as worn by Queen Elizabeth II.

RIGHT A close up of the accessories: pseudo-Faberge egg evening bag and ruby maharaja slippers.

Back detail: note the *couture*-like attention to detail of the origami-like folds in the fabric.

RIGHT A model walking in McQueen's Fall/Winter 2008 show wears a pristine crinoline paired with a luscious navy silk jacket, complementing the rich and vibrant reds dominating the collection whilst still maintaining the jewel tones characteristically associated with the Imperial Orient. Image courtesy of CATWALKING.COM

LEFT, AND DETAIL RIGHT A ballerina-like incarnation of the colonial theme on display at McQueen's Fall/Winter 2008 show. This model looks to be stepping out onto the stage of a *Swan Lake* or *La Vie Boheme* rather than a runway and she exudes a delicate, doll-like femininity which is often difficult to identify in McQueen's work. This look was accessorized with millions of dollars' worth of borrowed antique diamond neckpieces and Indian diadems, perfecting the imperial illusion. Image (left) courtesy of CATWALKING.COM

Spring/Summer 2009

A model walks the runway at McQueen's environmentally-themed Spring/Summer 2009 catwalk show. The set featured a giant image of the Earth projected, revolving on its axis, and a runway lined with a stuffed assortment of endangered species. McQueen wrote in his show notes that he had drawn inspiration from Charles Darwin's *Theory of Evolution* coupled with the destructive force of man's industrialization and the toll it is taking on the Earth. The collection's colourful prints, rendered in leggings, shifts and other accessible shapes such as the one pictured here, were, unlike much of McQueen's body of work over the years, an instant commercial success. Image courtesy of CATWALKING.COM

For Spring/Summer 2009, McQueen was amongst the first to flaunt such intricately detailed graphic prints on the runways of Paris, to use computer-enhanced technology to help him better realize his fantastical visions. Here, McQueen allows the print to take over the role of texture and tailoring; the perspective on the print is so poignant that the dress almost appears to be a living organism. Image courtesy of CATWALKING.COM

Here a model wears the same graphic print motif rendered in a jacket/ legging combination. The leggings ignited a craze for printed Lycra and were consequently repeated in subsequent collections as well as reproduced up and down the High Street.

RIGHT Detail from the back: the print mimics a spinal cord and the curve of the jacket's bustle the folded wings of a cicada or other airborne insect.

This sexy, sophisticated body-conscious shift, with its *trompe l'oeil* effect and sharply-padded shoulder, was a shape ahead of its time. Though this sort of exaggerated tailoring has always been a part of McQueen's *modus operandi*, this version is slightly more pared down and sets the stage for the trend explosion of shoulder-padded shifts the following season. Image courtesy of CATWALKING.COM

Fall/Winter 2009

Much like the eclecticsm of the Spring/ Summer 2008 collection, McQueen's Fall/ Winter 2009 collection was a patchwork of references to his own career as well as those of his major predecessors – pinching the houndstooth from Christian Dior's New Look here, and a bit of the classic Chanel tweed suit there, McQueen reworked these fashion milestones in a grotesque parody, which actually breathed new life into the antiquated staples. Philip Treacy again supplied outrageous headgear, and models appeared on the runway with half-comical, half-disturbing enormous black-painted lips.

The set of the Fall/Winter 2009 show embodied this notion of fragmentation, sartorial bits uprooted and recast to suit McQueen's macabre sense of humor and aesthetic, as the runway was surrounded by shattered bits of glass and discarded mechanical parts.

LEFT A model in a black quilted leather biker jacket wears a quasi-melted hubcap as a hat, another fantastical creation of the visionary milliner Philip Treacy for McQueen's Fall/Winter 2009 collection and example of McQueen's capability to envision beauty in even the most mundane, industrial of objects.

Amidst the citations of other designers, here McQueen again references his own work, with yet another incarnation of the bird theme. Philip Treacy has created a decadent birdcage headpiece, through which the aubergine plume-bedecked model peers out at the world.

Despite the theatrics of this design, the soft, pure white plumage in which the model is wrapped, like an infant swan, exudes a vulnerability so innocent, so pure despite the costume-element – another of McQueen's key aesthetic contradictions.

In direct contrast to the white swan, this model represents the harsher realities of the avian world, appearing as a crow or a fierce bird of prey in this enormous and threatening all-black feather concoction.

Here McQueen takes the fundamental elements of Dior's New Look and exaggerates them all. The enormous houndstooth bow coupled with the model's shaggy wig and enormous red pout is quite the parody of the quintessential Dior woman from the 1950s. However, exquisite tailoring with modern details ensures that the look is in fact much more than just an amusing reworking – classic McQueen tailoring in its own right.

McQueen extends the houndstooth treatment of the Fall/Winter 2009 collection to his elaborate footwear. Here the *geta* shoe shape has again been completely transformed into a calf-hugging soft lambskin boot.

RIGHT For this stunning evening look, McQueen executes a classic silhouette in an *avant-garde* graphic print. The chainmail sheath and mask, restored to the runway after a five year hiatus since its 2004 debut, is unexpectedly layered under the ready-to-red-carpet gown. The reinterpretation of this armoured top underscores his continual reworking of historical themes – of both his own personal history and of mankind globally.

Another show-stopping evening gown from the Autumn/Winter 2009 collection with a one-of-a-kind hat, again the result of a collaboration with Philip Treacy.

RIGHT The extreme *geta* recast from the Spring/Summer 2008 collection, this time a Mary Jane strap lends a touch of the European to the otherwise immediately-identifiably Japanese shape.

Spring/Summer 2010

LEFT Models take their final turn on the runway of McQueen's *Plato's Atlantis* show in Paris, the last at which he would ever take his final bow. Robotic cameras on enormous booms feeding the show live to the internet circled the sparkling, mother-of-pearl hued runway whilst the background boasted a giant screen playing a video of a naked model Raquel Zimmermann writhing on the sand, snakes slithering about her.

A model as a 'blue alien' walks the runway at McQueen's Spring/Summer 2010 show. This ultra-mini, super-structured reptile-skin-patterned dress is particularly representative of the collection and underscores McQueen's perfected technique of digital printing. Each dress was a hybrid of computer-generated images with McQueen's *couture*-based signature cuts, the perfect marriage of man and machine in an innovative fashion context. Image courtesy of CATWALKING.COM

The model's hand-embellished top has an organic feeling, almost as though she is an insect and the garment her hardened outer shell. The intricacy of the bell-sleeved top has a couture-like drama and is contrasted simply with a tie-dye silk mini-skirt.

One of the strongest features of the *Plato's Atlantis* collection is its outrageous footwear, which made headlines around the world. Pictured here are the 'monster' stilettos, melted and twisted plastic meant to evoke a post-nuclear-apocalyptic landscape after the ecological meltdown of the planet.

The famous 'Armadillo' shoes shocked fashion insiders and the general public alike. These twelve-inch python stilettos literally stole the show despite the fact that several models refused to step out onto the runway in them, for fear of breaking a leg.

A silhouetted Alexander McQueen, almost larger-than-life, appears
at the head of the runway for his finale bow for the last time at the
end of the *Plato's Atlantis* Spring/Summer 2010 show in Paris.

CONCLUSION

Alexander McQueen's parting gift to the fashion world was his Fall/Winter 2010 collection. It showed in small presentations to groups of about ten editors at a time on March 9, 2010, and had the somber feel of a requiem to a great artist fallen rather than a showcase of fashion design. Staged in the private gilded salons of Paris' Hôtel de Clermont-Tonnerre, family headquarters of PPR (which owns Gucci Group and hence, the McQueen label), the presentations were a highly private affair – a goodbye.

Only sixteen pieces were shown, which were 80% complete at the time of McQueen's death. Sarah Burton, McQueen's right-hand designer for the past decade, took on the challenge of bringing her creative director's final vision to three-dimensional fruition in the salons of Paris.

In an eerily prophetic manner, the collection was weighted with a spiritual seriousness – referencing Baroque aesthetics of gilding and decadent embellishment as well as the ornamental beauty of medieval art – whilst simultaneously self-referencing McQueen's own milestone collections past. It was a *tour de force* of the longevity of his talent as well as his parting message, spelled out across 16 sets of exquisitely-crafted *couture*-like garments.

Steeped in religious iconography, one model, dressed in a full-length white chiffon gown worn underneath a floor-length hand-embellished robe, seemed to float across the floor, an angel from a 14th-century altarpiece made real. Another, in a body-hugging hooded digital-printed evening column, glowed like an archangel carved from marble gazing gently down from the nave of some grand cathedral. Works by Byzantine artists Jean Fouquet, Sandro Botticelli, Stephan Lochner, Grinling Gibbons (whose master woodcarvings adorn St. Paul's Cathedral in London) and Hieronymus Bosch were digitally recreated in their entirety and printed onto heavy silk in rich cardinal reds and hand-embellished with what looked like gold leaf.

The final look – a fitted high-collared jacket made of feathers hand-dipped in gold paint over a full white skirt with gold filigree detailing about the hem – had about it a heavenly serenity executed with *couture* capability. The use of feathers and the bird reference, one of the many signatures McQueen developed over his career, here seemed to suggest a sort of immortal finality.

While Lee Alexander McQueen himself may no longer be laying the plumes in place, strapping his models into corsets so restrictive they faint, and shocking us season after season with his runway spectacles, his legacy, a design aesthetic so fully submerged in his vision, has eclipsed the designer's own imagination and become a kind of fashion religion itself.

The members of its church, his devoted fans and costumers, will continue to be led by the team of disciples who have stood by his side over the last decade and a half. McQueen's work lives on. Beyond domination of the mortal world – his proclaimed interest at the time of his Spring/Summer 2010 show – with this final collection just one season later, McQueen looks towards conquering the immortal one. The man behind the myth has transcended into sartorial sainthood and will hold a revered place in the fashion canon as long as models continue to storm the runway.

A model presents one of the sixteen looks from McQueen's final Autumn/Winter 2010 collection in Paris. The gilded brocade bodice speaks of McQueen's obsession with historical reference in his pattern cutting. The pleated mini-skirt balances out the stiffness of the ornate top and keeps the look quizzically young and modern. Image courtesy of CATWALKING.COM

RIGHT Perhaps an insight into the designer's psyche in those final days, this look is literally stamped with an unmissable yet equally unsettling rumination on the afterlife; the bodice of the dress is printed with a scene from Hieronymus Bosch's late 16th-century triptych *The Garden of Earthly Delights*. Made using state-of-the-art printing and textile technologies, the focus of this print is solely the Old Master's imagining of the torments of Hell and not his renditions of the Garden of Eden with Adam and Eve or depiction of the garden of earthly delights, which make up the other two panels of the triptych. Image courtesy of CATWALKING.COM

This ornate and exquisite full-length hand-embroidered and hand-embellished gown teamed with cape is a *couture*-level statement piece on par in its construction with the traditional costume of a Byzantine empress. The extraordinary attention to handcrafted workmanship and detail executed across a canvas of a relatively straightforwardly cut garment, simplistic in its clean lines, is in stark contrast with McQueen's futuristic digital-print-ridden Spring/Summer 2010 *Plato's Atlantis* collection. Image courtesy of CATWALKING.COM

This look, simplistic in cut, yet exquisite in silver-embroidered detail, radiates the ethereal beauty of an angel as depicted in traditional Catholic imagery. The model's head is bound with bandages, a move which at once references McQueen's legendary Spring/Summer 2001 *Asylum* collection whilst also nodding towards the head coverings donned by modest women in Northen European medieval and Renaissance portraiture, such as Johannes Vermeer's 1665 masterpiece, *Girl with a Pearl Earring*. Image courtesy of CATWALKING.COM

The final look from Alexander McQueen's final collection is one of optimism and hope. After a collection touching on various medieval incarnations of the afterlife, including Bosch's fiendish conception of Hell, this final gown and golden feathered jacket seems to offer the audience a beacon of light and pure beauty. In keeping with McQueen's love of avian imagery, this figure appears to be an angelic dove, a glorious apparition, ready to take wing and return to the side of her creator. Image courtesy of CATWALKING. COM